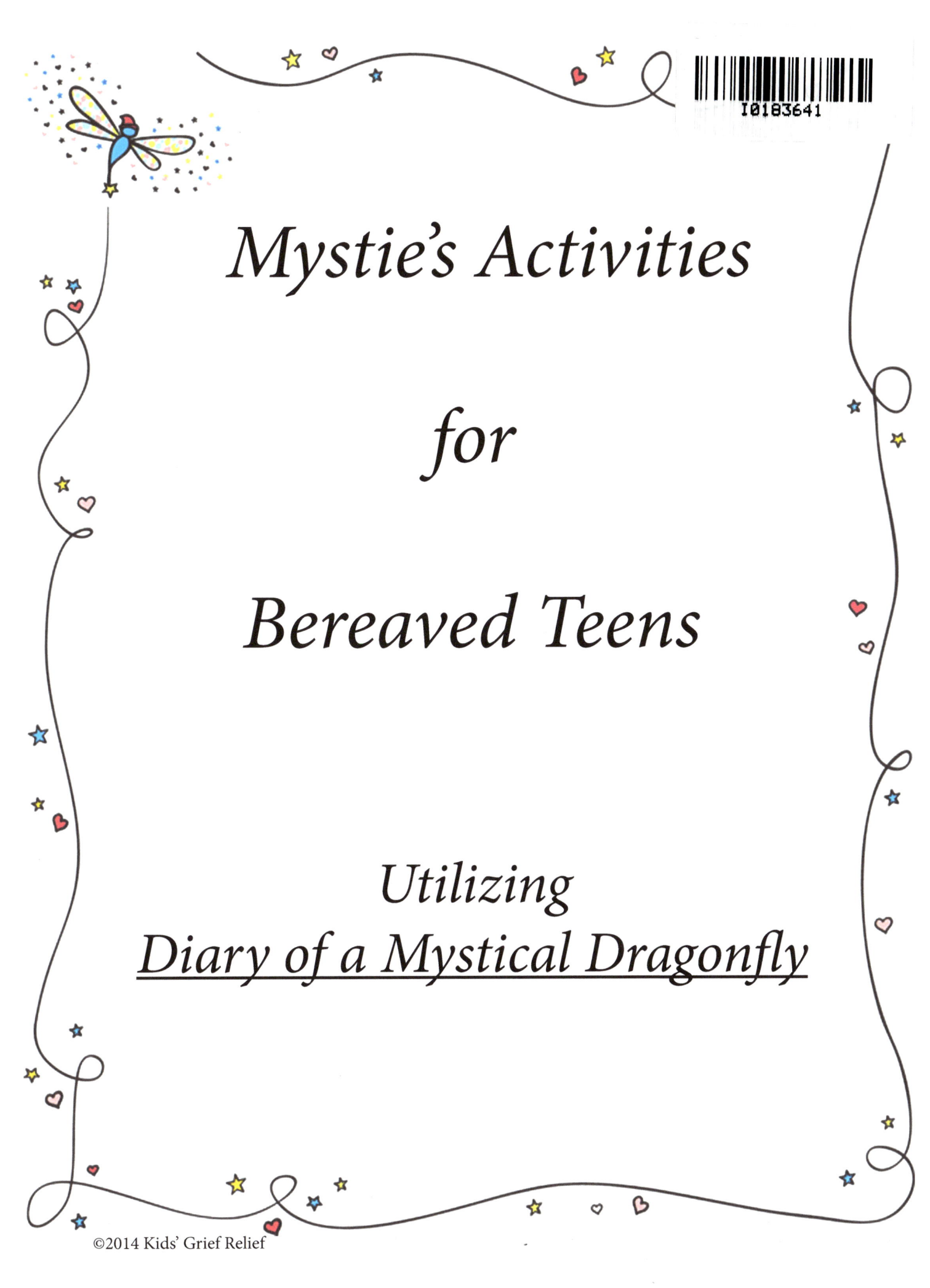

Mystie's Activities for Bereaved Teens

Utilizing *Diary of a Mystical Dragonfly*

©2014 Kids' Grief Relief

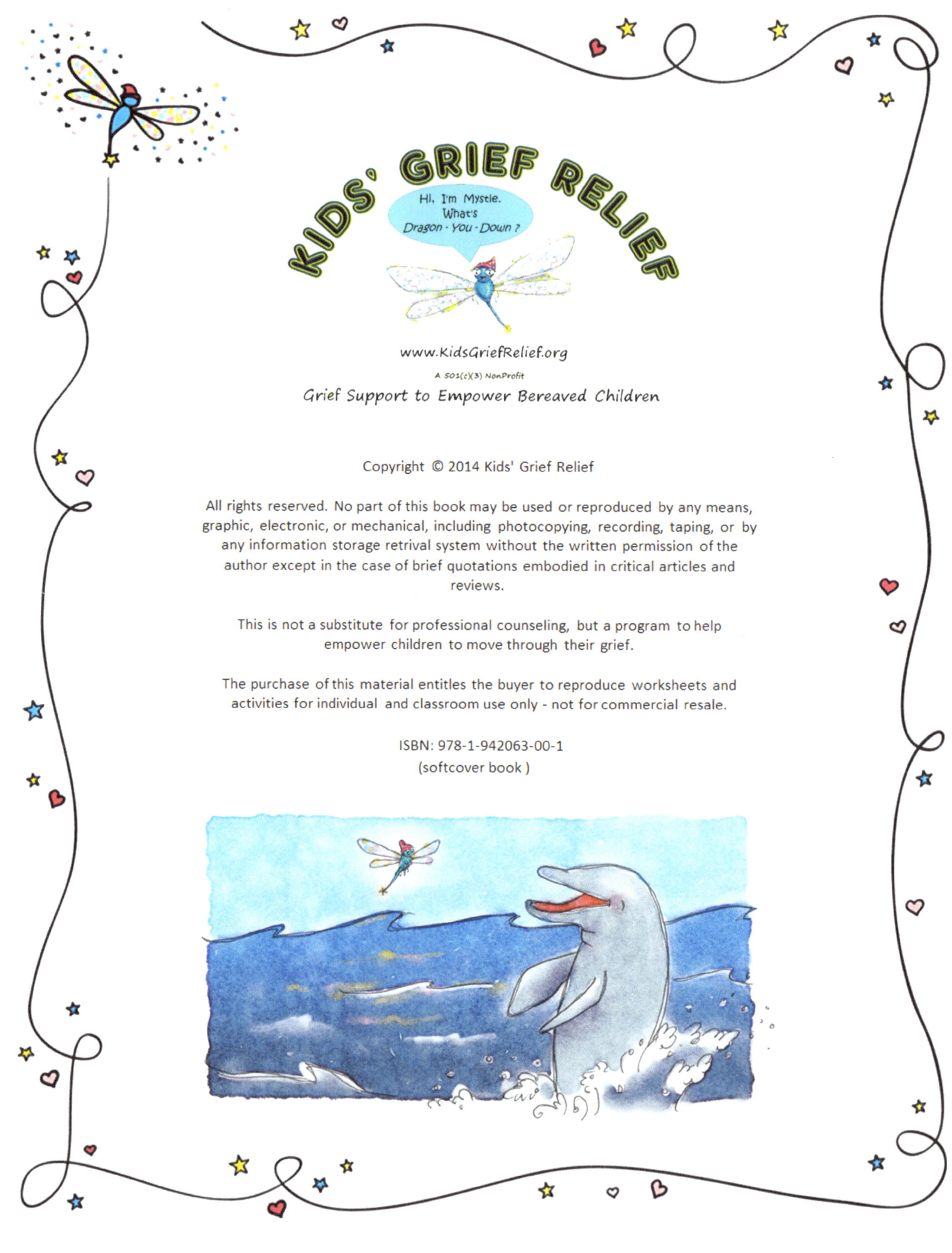

MY FAMILY MEMBERS

Circle the ones you live with

My special person who died: _____

Activity 2

What goes on in my Grief Support Group, stays in my Grief Support Group.

signed_____

date_____

Who is in my Grief Support Group?

Activity 2   ©2014 Kids' Grief Relief

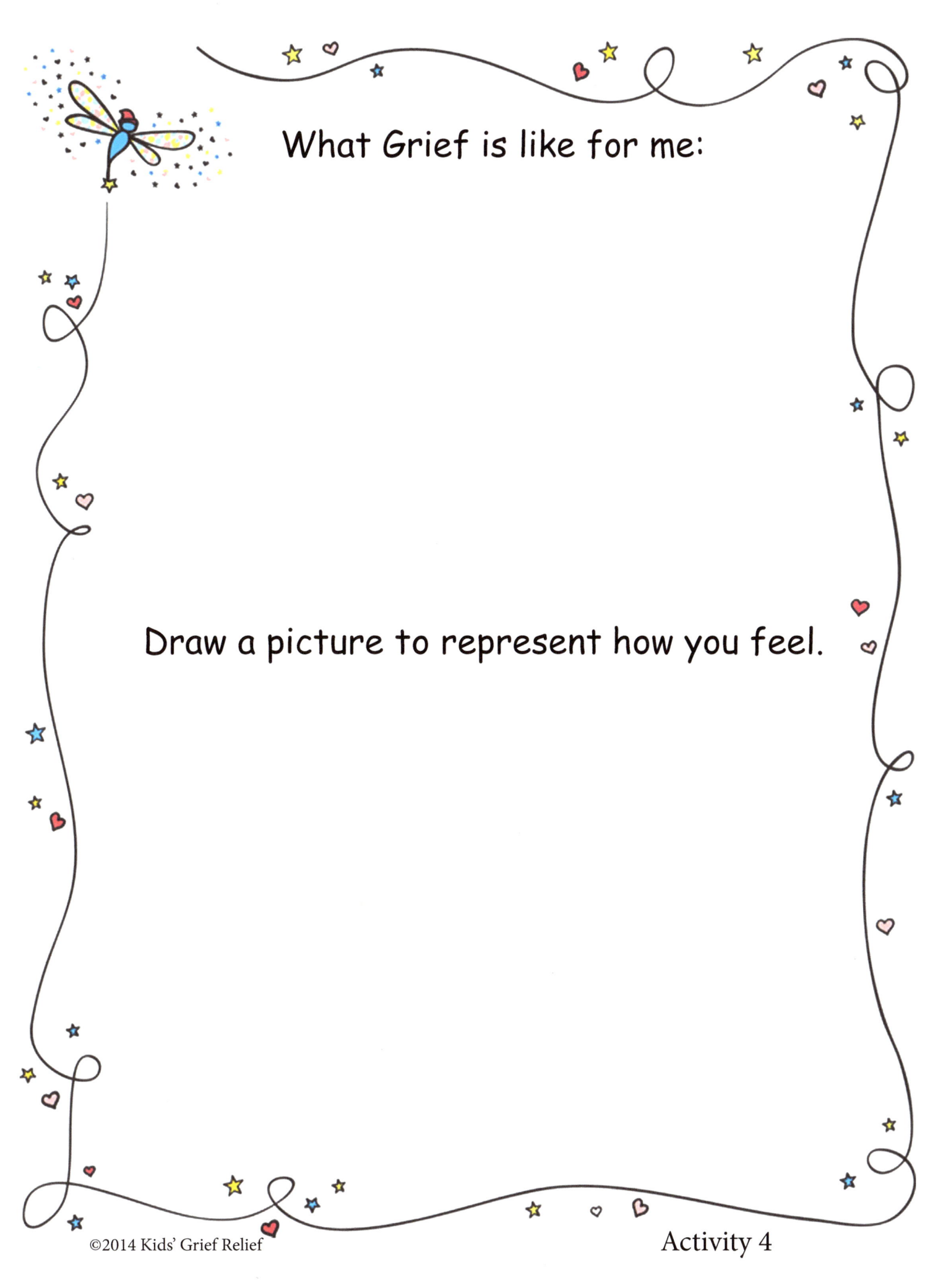

What Grief is like for me:

Draw a picture to represent how you feel.

THERE IS NO "RIGHT WAY" TO GRIEVE.

YOU ARE GRIEVING THE WAY YOU NEED TO.

Other people who are grieving over the death of my loved one:

_____
_____
_____

People who are supporting me:

_____
_____
_____
_____

You've had many experiences throughout your life. Which ones do you always want to remember?

Write down at least five different memories that mean something to you.

This timeline ends with the death of your loved one. You will have an opportunity to add to your timeline in another lesson.

MY TIMELINE

Birth — Started School — Death of Loved One

Age

As you listen to others share their timeline, notice how different some of your memories are from the other students in your group.

Also notice that some are the same as others.

Activity 8 ©2014 Kids' Grief Relief

It's important to tell your story about the death of your loved one.

What happened is part of your life forever.

It's unique.

WRITE YOUR STORY ON THE NEXT PAGE USING THE PROMPTS BELOW

- Tell something about the relationship you had with your loved one before he/she died.

- What was your relationship like just before he/she died?"

- Tell about the day your loved one died. Where were you? How did you find out? Who was with you? Where did you go? How did you feel?

- Tell about the memorial service for your loved one. Was there a funeral? Did you participate? Was your loved one cremated? If so, where are the ashes?

- How did the rest of your family and friends react to the death?

- What was the worst part of the experience?

1 What is the first and last name of your special person?	**2** Did your special person teach you anything?	**3** Do you know your special person's birthday? (Day/Month/Year)	**4** Was your special person buried or cremated?	**5** Did your special person like to wear jewelry? What kind?
6 Describe a special holiday spent with your special person.	**7** Tell about the last time you saw your special person.	**8** What name did your special person call you?	**9** Tell about a funny moment with your special person.	**10** Describe a trip you took with your special person.
11 Tell about what kind of clothes your special person liked to wear.	**12** Tell about an object that reminds you of your special person.	**13** What kind of music did your special person enjoy?	**14** What kind of movies did your special person like to watch?	**15** Did your special person ever have a pet?
16 Did your special person have a favorite saying - what was it?	**17** Tell about a sad memory with your favorite person.	**18** Tell about some of the people who loved your special person.	**19** What one thing always makes you think about your special person?	**20** What's your favorite photo of your special person? Describe it.
21 Tell about something your special person loved to do.	**22** What time of day do you feel "dragged-down" over the death of your special person?	**23** What's the one thing you will miss MOST about your special person?	**24** Do you feel peaceful about the way your special person was buried? Why?	**25** Tell about a gift you gave your special person.

©2014 Kids' Grief Relief

Activity 13

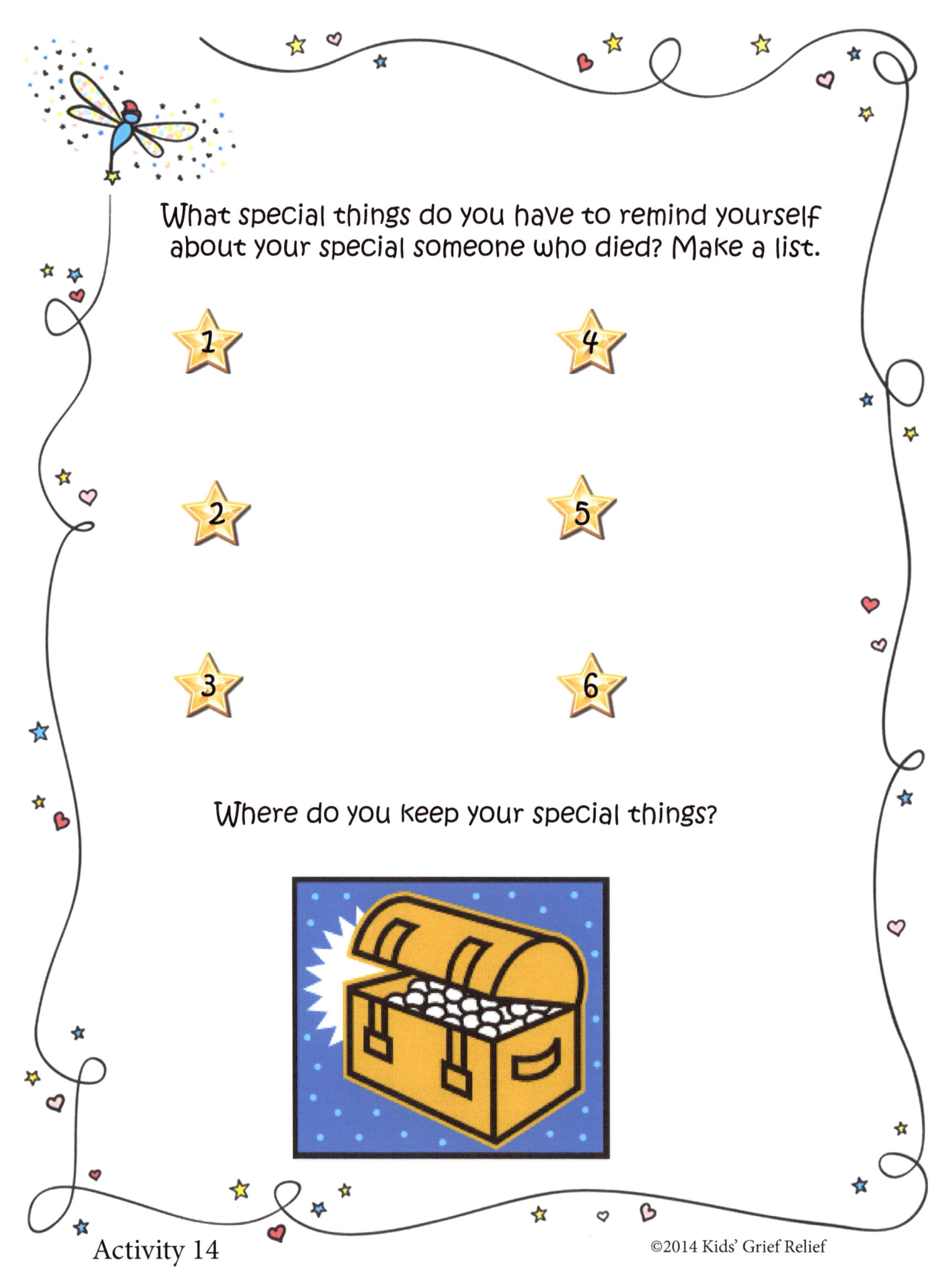

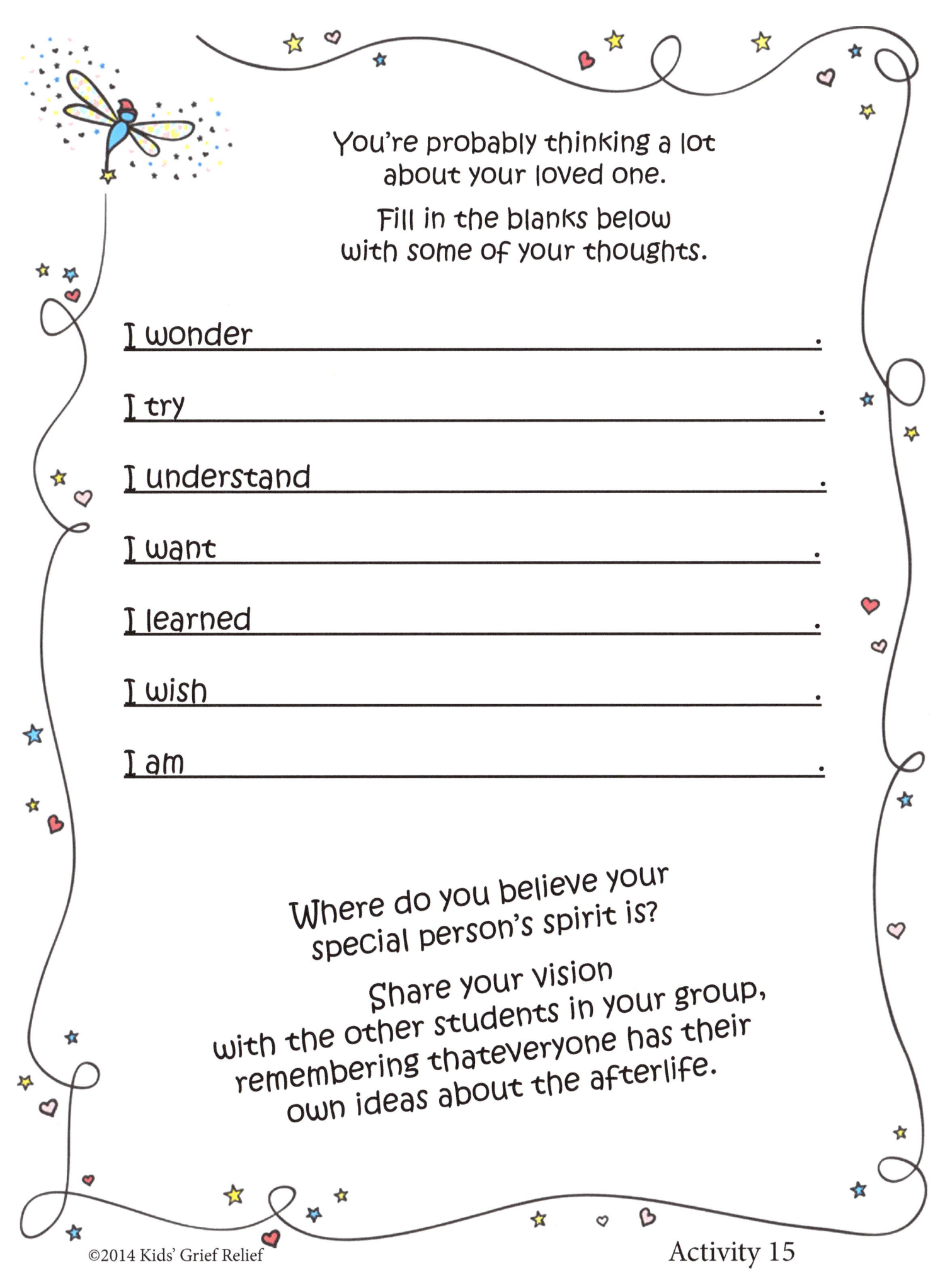

Activity 18

Chapter One
I Am A Mystical Dragonfly

On a scale of 1 to 5,
with 5 meaning you completely <u>agree</u>,
and 1 meaning you completely <u>disagree</u>,
rate your thoughts and feelings about these statements.

1. I like my name. _____
   (1-5)

2. I remember a lot about my childhood. _____
   (1-5)

3. I know what my "inner spirit"/ "inner self" is. _____
   (1-5)

4. My life is important. _____
   (1-5)

5. I have something special to share with the world. _____
   (1-5)

Chapter Two
I Grow My Wings

Rate Yourself:

1. Even though I don't always act like it, I believe my true nature is Love._____
   (1-5)

2. I am aware of what I am thinking most of the time._____
   (1-5)

3. I am aware of how my thoughts and feelings help to create my experience. _____
   (1-5)

4. I don't allow myself to get distracted when I choose to achieve something._____
   (1-5)

5. I learn from my mistakes._____
   (1-5)

Chapter Three
I Fly To Earth

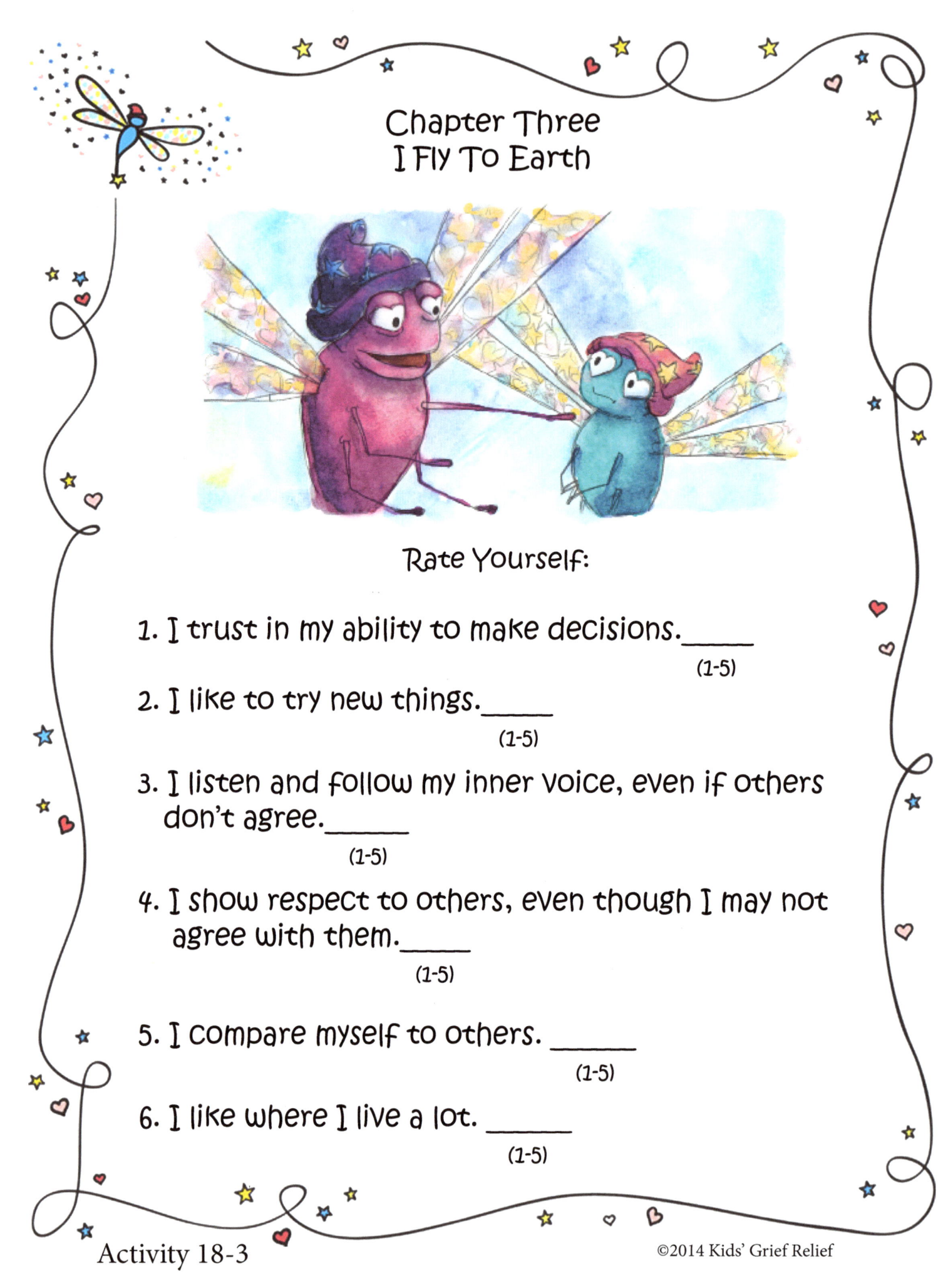

Rate Yourself:

1. I trust in my ability to make decisions. _____
   (1-5)

2. I like to try new things. _____
   (1-5)

3. I listen and follow my inner voice, even if others don't agree. _____
   (1-5)

4. I show respect to others, even though I may not agree with them. _____
   (1-5)

5. I compare myself to others. _____
   (1-5)

6. I like where I live a lot. _____
   (1-5)

Chapter Four
My Best Friend Darvy

Rate Yourself:

1. I make friends easily. _____
   (1-5)

2. I accept people the way they are. _____
   (1-5)

3. I like how I look. _____
   (1-5)

4. I feel comfortable around all kinds of people. _____
   (1-5)

5. I express gratitude to the important people in my life. _____
   (1-5)

6. I think about my friends/family dying. _____
   (1-5)

7. It's NOT FAIR that some people die young. _____
   (1-5)

Chapter Five
Darvy's Funeral

Rate Yourself:

1. I have been to funerals, and I think they are a good way to honor someone's life. _____
(1-5)

2. I remember the worst part of the funeral. _____
(1-5)

3. I remember the best part of the funeral. _____
(1-5)

4. I feel comfortable with people being buried in caskets. _____
(1-5)

5. I feel comfortable with people/pets being cremated. _____
(1-5)

6. I feel comfortable when I visit a cemetary. _____
(1-5)

7. I feel comfortable talking about death._____
(1-5)

Chapter Six
What Grandpa Was Talking About

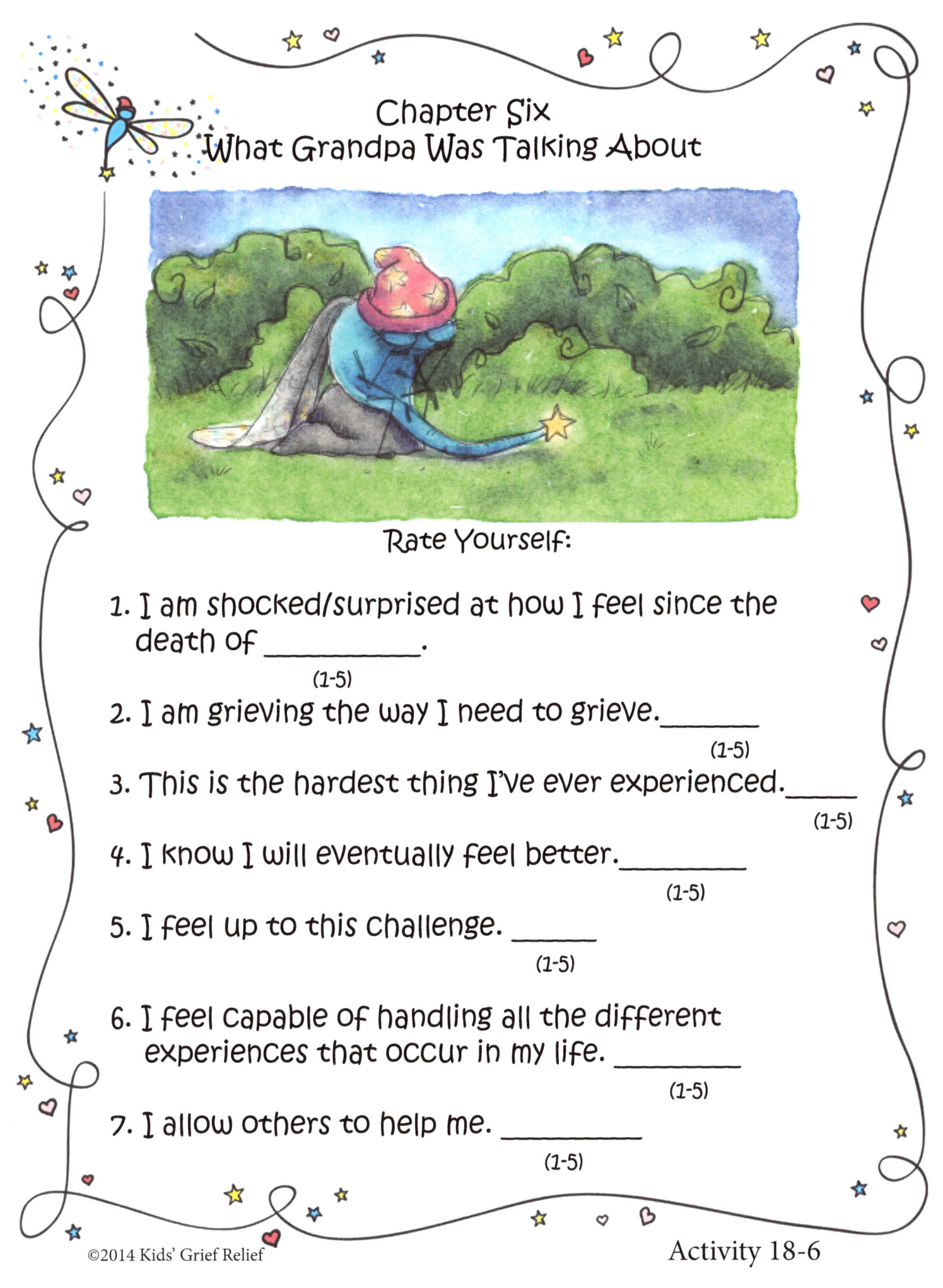

Rate Yourself:

1. I am shocked/surprised at how I feel since the death of _____.
   (1-5)

2. I am grieving the way I need to grieve. _____
   (1-5)

3. This is the hardest thing I've ever experienced. ____
   (1-5)

4. I know I will eventually feel better. _____
   (1-5)

5. I feel up to this challenge. _____
   (1-5)

6. I feel capable of handling all the different experiences that occur in my life. _____
   (1-5)

7. I allow others to help me. _____
   (1-5)

©2014 Kids' Grief Relief

Activity 18-6

Chapter Seven
It's Time To Go Home!

Rate Yourself:

1. I have learned something new about myself. _____
   (1-5)

2. I have learned something new about life. _____
   (1-5)

3. Knowing every "thing" is impermanent or temporary has changed my outlook on life. _____
   (1-5)

4. I now can help others who are grieving. _____
   (1-5)

5. I know what my greatest strength is. _____
   (1-5)

6. I use my intuition to help solve some of my problems. _____
   (1-5)

7. The character in the story who best represents me is _____.

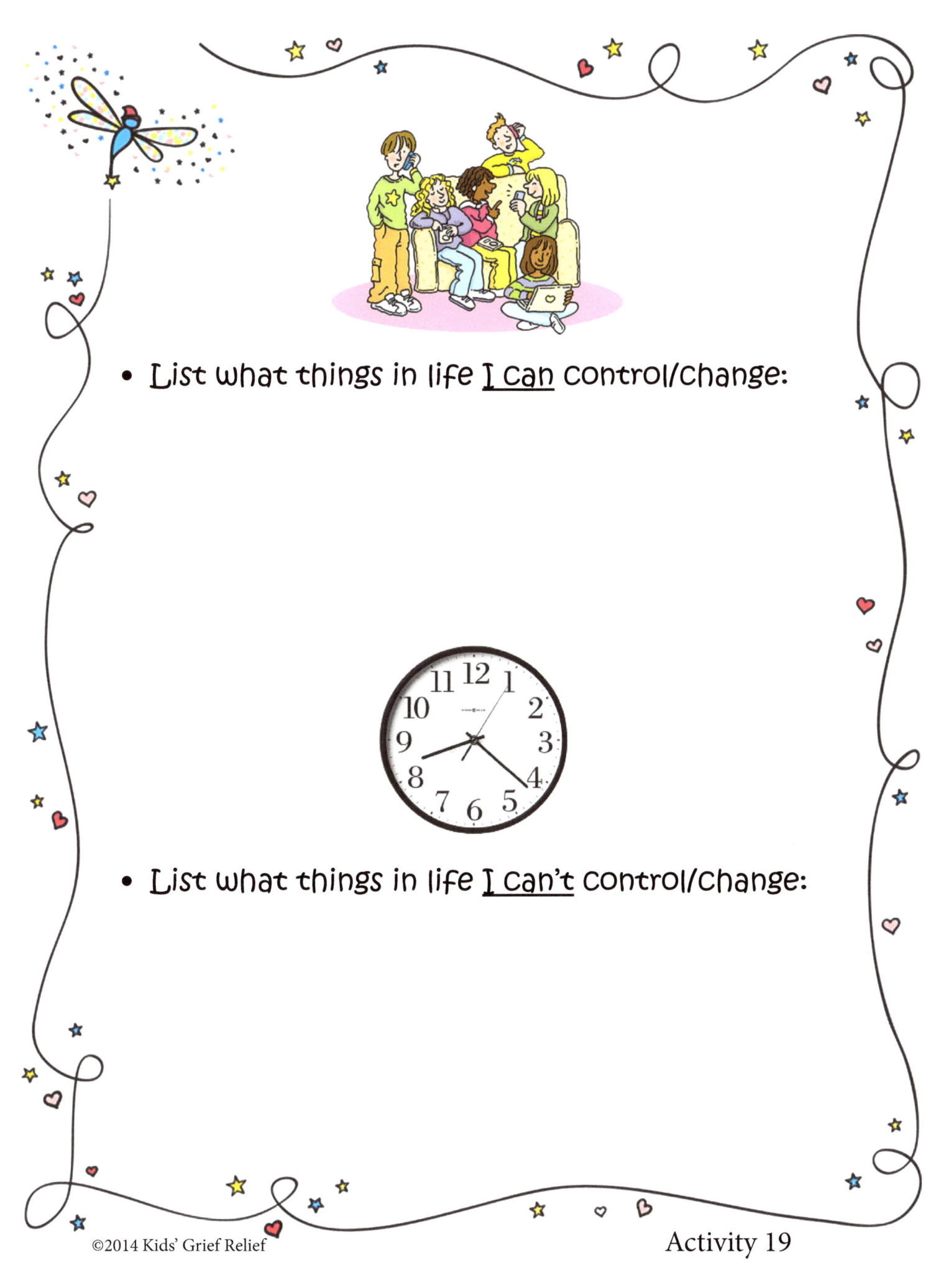

- List what things in life <u>I can</u> control/change:

- List what things in life <u>I can't</u> control/change:

Activity 19

WHAT YOU THINK MATTERS

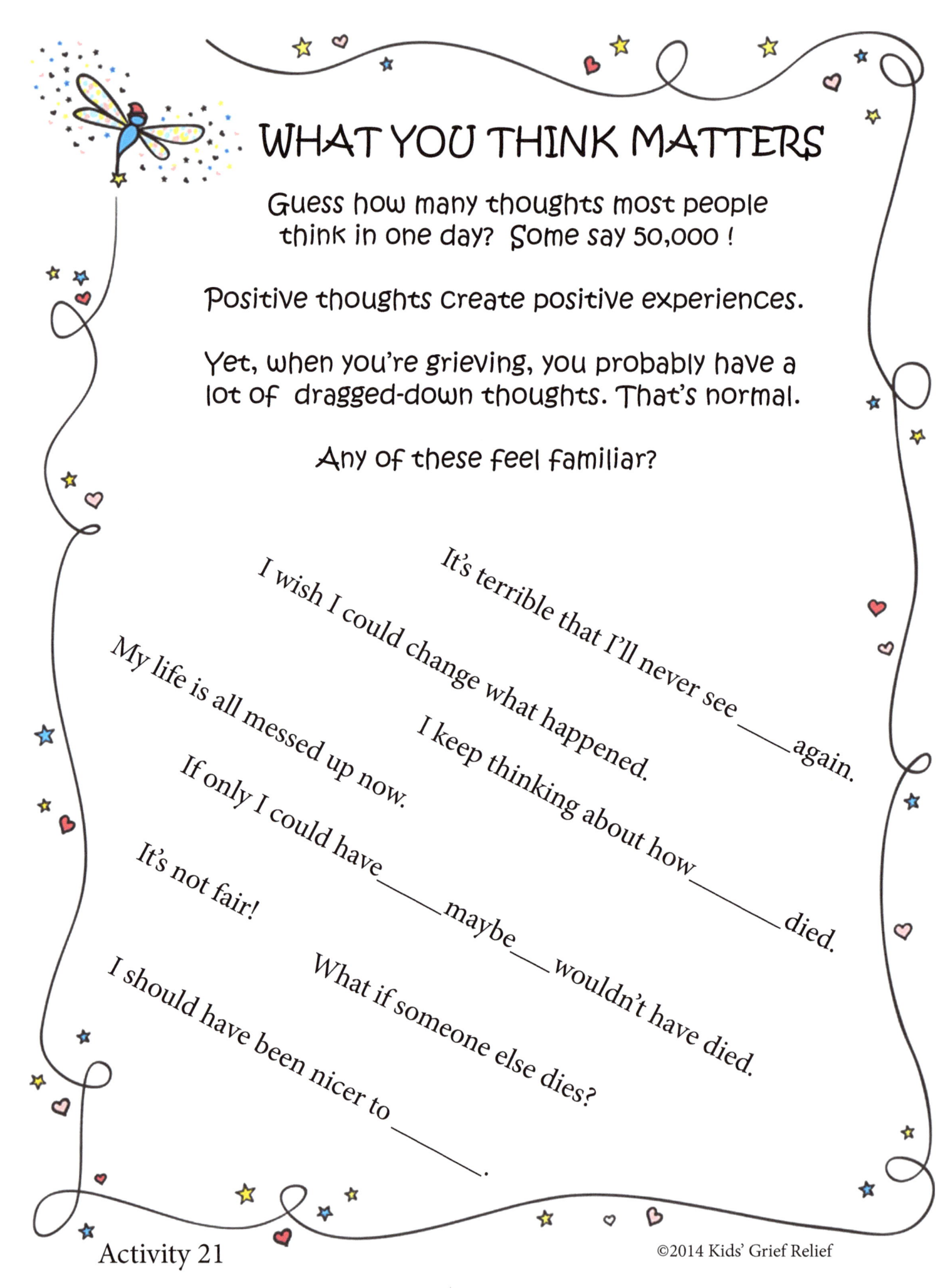

Guess how many thoughts most people think in one day? Some say 50,000!

Positive thoughts create positive experiences.

Yet, when you're grieving, you probably have a lot of dragged-down thoughts. That's normal.

Any of these feel familiar?

It's terrible that I'll never see _____ again.

I wish I could change what happened.

My life is all messed up now.

I keep thinking about how _____ died.

If only I could have _____ maybe _____ wouldn't have died.

It's not fair!

What if someone else dies?

I should have been nicer to _____.

Activity 21 ©2014 Kids' Grief Relief

1. I am brave.

2. I am smart enough to understand what happened.

3. It feels good to talk to others about what happened.

4. I have my own unique feelings about death.

5. I have special memories of _____ that I will always treasure.

6. I like who I am.

7. I am grateful for all the people who love me.

8. I am a powerful kid!

9. I can find healthy ways to let go of anger.

10. I am capable to handle what's going on in my life.

11. I choose relationships with people who appreciate me for who I am.

Dear _____

Love Always,

_____

Activity 25A

©2014 Kids' Grief Relief

Dear _____

_____
_____
_____
_____
_____
_____
_____
_____
_____
_____
_____
_____

Love Always,

_____

©2014 Kids' Grief Relief

Activity 25B

FOREVER CALENDAR

During each and every day,
We Love them.

During each and every night,
We Love them.

During each and every week,
We Love them.

During each and every month,
We Love them.

During each and every season,
We Love them.

During each and every year,
We Love them.

As the days turn into weeks, turn into months,
turn into seasons, turn into years,
We Love them;
Forever.

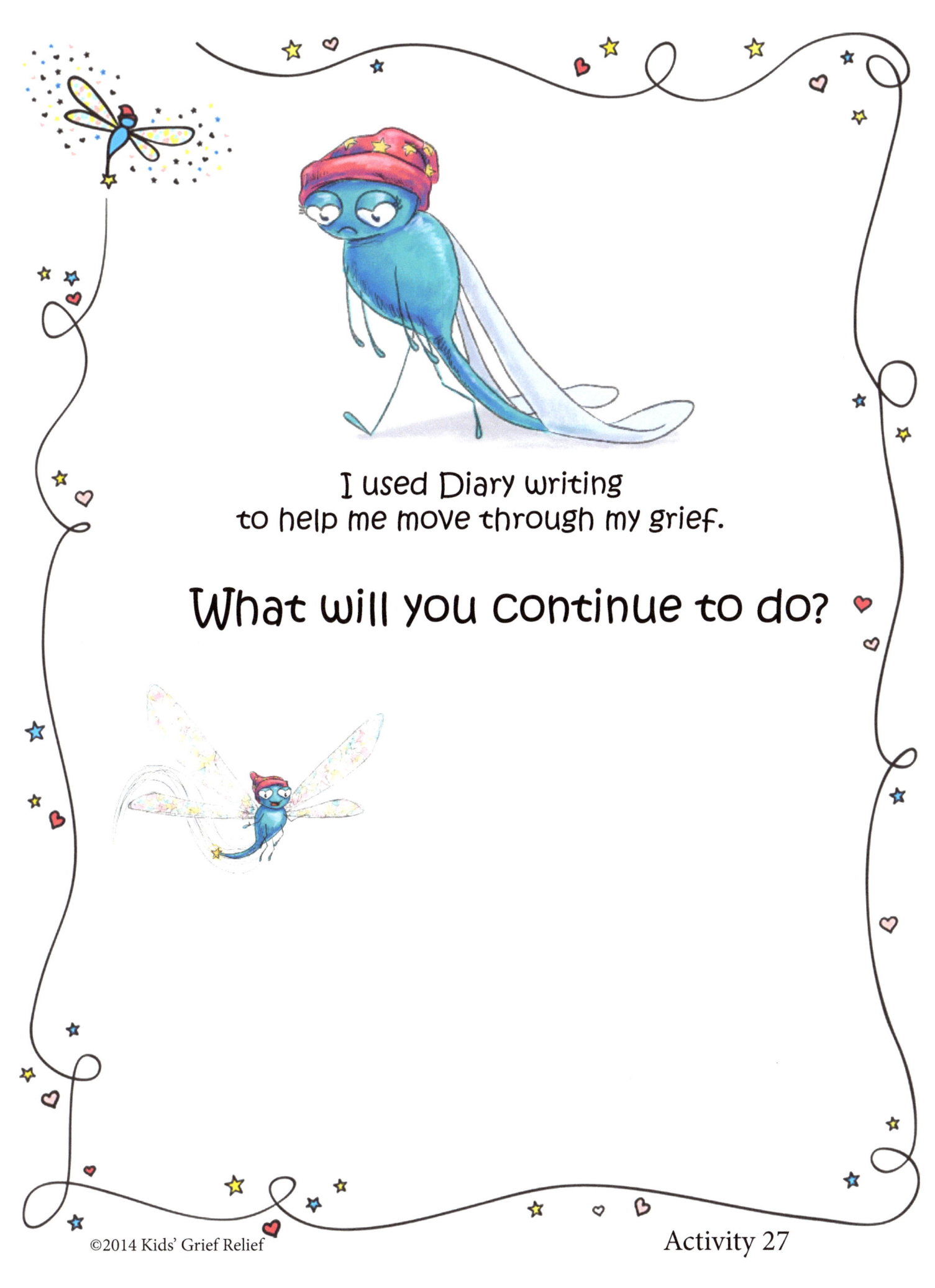

www.ingramcontent.com/pod-product-compliance
Lightning Source LLC
LaVergne TN
LVHW072127070426
835512LV00002B/35